# Welcome to EmpowerHer Soul

Welcome, beautiful soul! Thank you for opening this book and giving yourself permission to embrace a journey of self-love, empowerment, and creativity. EmpowerHER Soul was designed with you in mind – a strong, resilient Black woman who deserves to take time for herself, nurture her spirit, and celebrate the beauty within.

In these pages, you'll find powerful imagery and affirmations created to inspire, uplift, and remind you of your worth. Each page is an invitation to reconnect with the parts of yourself that are often hidden or forgotten in the hustle of daily life. As you color, reflect, and engage with these pages, let each image serve as a mirror to your inner strength, beauty, and light.

This book is more than a coloring book; it's a safe space to be yourself, feel yourself, and celebrate yourself. Through each theme – whether it's resilience, joy, healing, or self-worth – my hope is that you find encouragement, peace, and a sense of connection to the amazing woman you are.

**How to Use This Book**

- **Set Aside Time for You:** Give yourself permission to color and reflect without distractions. Even a few quiet minutes can help you recharge and realign.

- **Let Your Colors Flow:** Don't worry about creating a perfect picture; instead, let each color choice reflect how you feel in the moment.

- **Reflect on Each Affirmation:** Each page has been paired with affirmations or prompts to inspire deeper self-connection. Take a moment to read, reflect, and feel each word.

- **Express Yourself Fully:** These pages are here to support your journey, whether you're celebrating a triumph or need a gentle reminder of your strength.

As you move through this book, know that you are not alone. You're part of a community of empowered Black women choosing to love themselves, embrace their unique journeys, and honor the beautiful complexity within. So grab your favorite colors, take a deep breath, and enjoy the beautiful journey of self-discovery and self-love that lies ahead.
With love and empowerment,

The EmpowerHER Team

Copyright © 2024
All rights reserved.

All rights reserved. No part of this publication, including the characters, and artwork, may be reproduced, distributed, or transmitted in any form or by any means, electronic or mechanical, without the prior written permission of the copyright owner. Unauthorized copying, reproduction, or distribution of this book is strictly prohibited.

This coloring book is intended for personal use only. It is not permitted to use the content of this book for commercial purposes, such as selling or mass reproducing the artwork or activities. The purchase of this book grants the buyer the right to use it for personal enjoyment and non-commercial purposes.

Please respect the copyright of the author, as well as the intellectual property rights associated with the content of this book. Thank you for your understanding and cooperation.

©2024 | Infinite Source Corporation  All Rights Reserved

# COLOR TEST

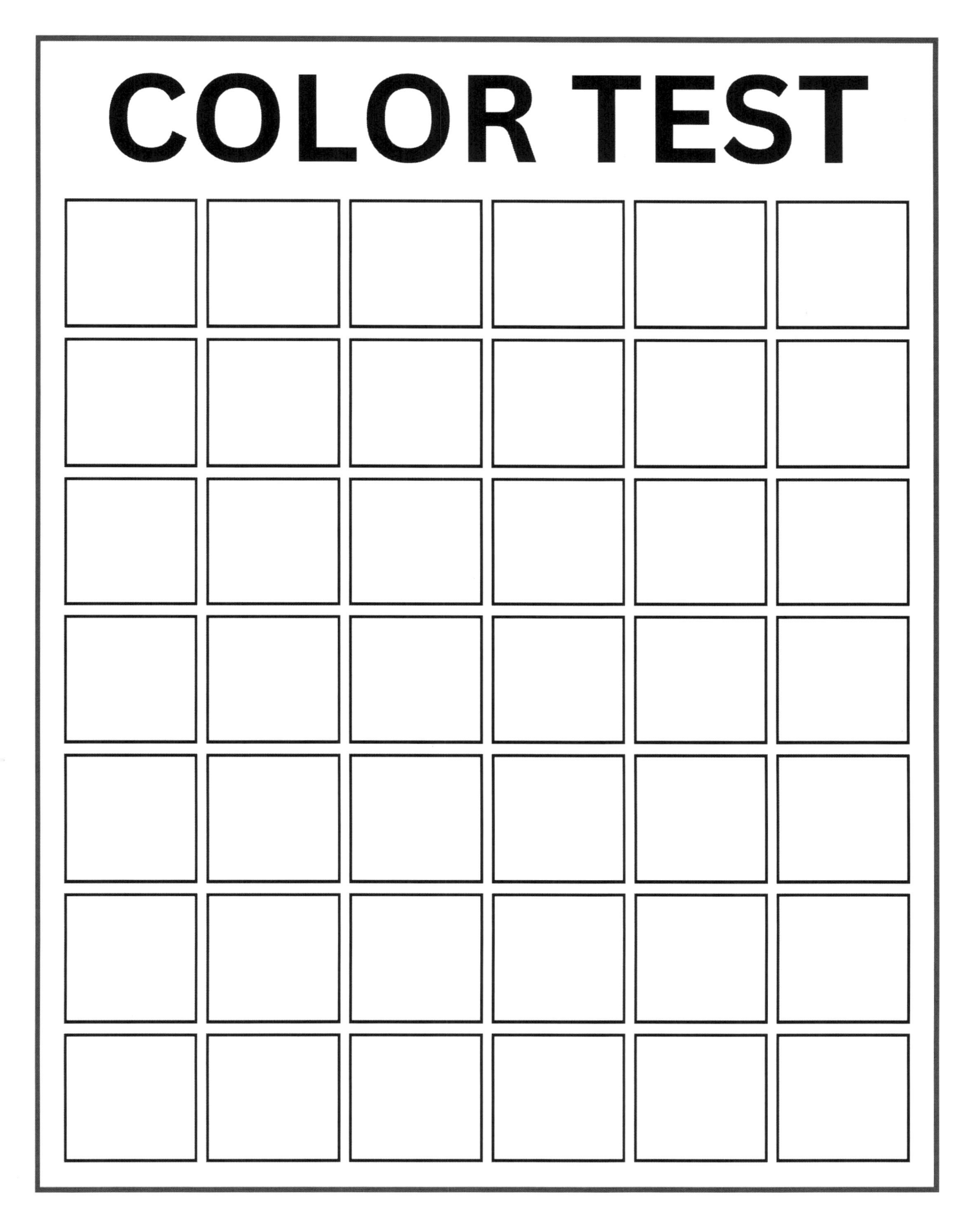

# I am worthy of my own love and admiration

# Self Love

What makes me unique, and how can I celebrate it today?

# I accept myself for who I am

I AM  ENOUGH

Self-love is not about perfection; it's about appreciating yourself exactly as you are

# I embrace every part of me with love and gratitude

# Self-Care Tips

✓ **Practice Daily Affirmations:** Begin each day by speaking loving words to yourself in the mirror. Remind yourself, "I am worthy of love and respect."

✓ **Create a Self-Care Ritual:** Dedicate a specific time each week to pamper yourself, whether through a spa day at home, journaling, or simply taking a walk.

✓ **Set Boundaries:** Learn to say "no" without guilt and prioritize your well-being by creating healthy boundaries with others.

# I am my own greatest love story

# Resilience

How have I shown resilience in my life, and what qualities helped me?

# I have the strength to overcome anything

# Self-Care Tips

- ✓ **Embrace Challenges as Lessons:** See setbacks as opportunities for growth rather than failures. Reflect on how they can make you stronger.

- ✓ **Surround Yourself with Support:** Lean on your trusted circle of friends and mentors who uplift you during difficult times.

- ✓ **Cultivate a Growth Mindset:** When faced with obstacles, remind yourself, "I am capable of overcoming anything that comes my way."

# I carry myself with pride and self-assurance

# CONFIDENCE

What are my unique strengths, and how can I show them to the world?

# I trust myself and proudly step into my power

# Self-Care Tips

✓ **Celebrate Small Wins:** Take note of your accomplishments, no matter how small, and acknowledge your progress regularly.

✓ **Stand Tall and Speak Up:** Practice confident body language and speak with conviction to reflect your inner strength.

✓ **Challenge Negative Self-Talk:** Replace self-doubt with empowering statements like, "I believe in myself and my abilities."

# I welcome growth, change, and transformation

# Growth & Transformation

In what ways have I grown recently,
and what am I ready to learn?

# I am growing beautifully, in my own time

Growth is not about rushing forward; it's about taking each step with intention and openness

# I am thankful for my journey and all it brings

# Self-Care Tips

✓ Commit to Lifelong Learning: Read, take classes, or explore new experiences to keep growing and evolving.

✓ Reflect Regularly: Take time to review your personal progress and identify areas for continued growth.

✓ Step Out of Your Comfort Zone: Challenge yourself with new experiences that push your boundaries.

# I am constantly evolving and becoming my best self

Evolving
Learning
Acceptance

# Manifestation and Abundance

What are my dreams and desires, and how can I align my energy and actions to bring them into reality?

# What I am seeking is seeking me

"Abundance is not something we acquire; it's something we tune into."

— Wayne Dyer

# I am worthy of all the abundance in my life

# Self-Care Tips

✓ **Practice Gratitude Daily:** Begin each day by acknowledging the abundance already present in your life. Write down three things you're grateful for to set a positive tone.

✓ **Visualize Your Goals:** Take a few minutes each day to close your eyes and imagine yourself living the life you desire. Visualize every detail and feel the emotions of having achieved it.

✓ **Declutter Your Space:** Clear out physical and mental clutter to make room for new blessings. Create an environment that reflects openness and abundance.

# I am on a path uniquely designed for me; I trust my journey

# Inner Peace and Calm

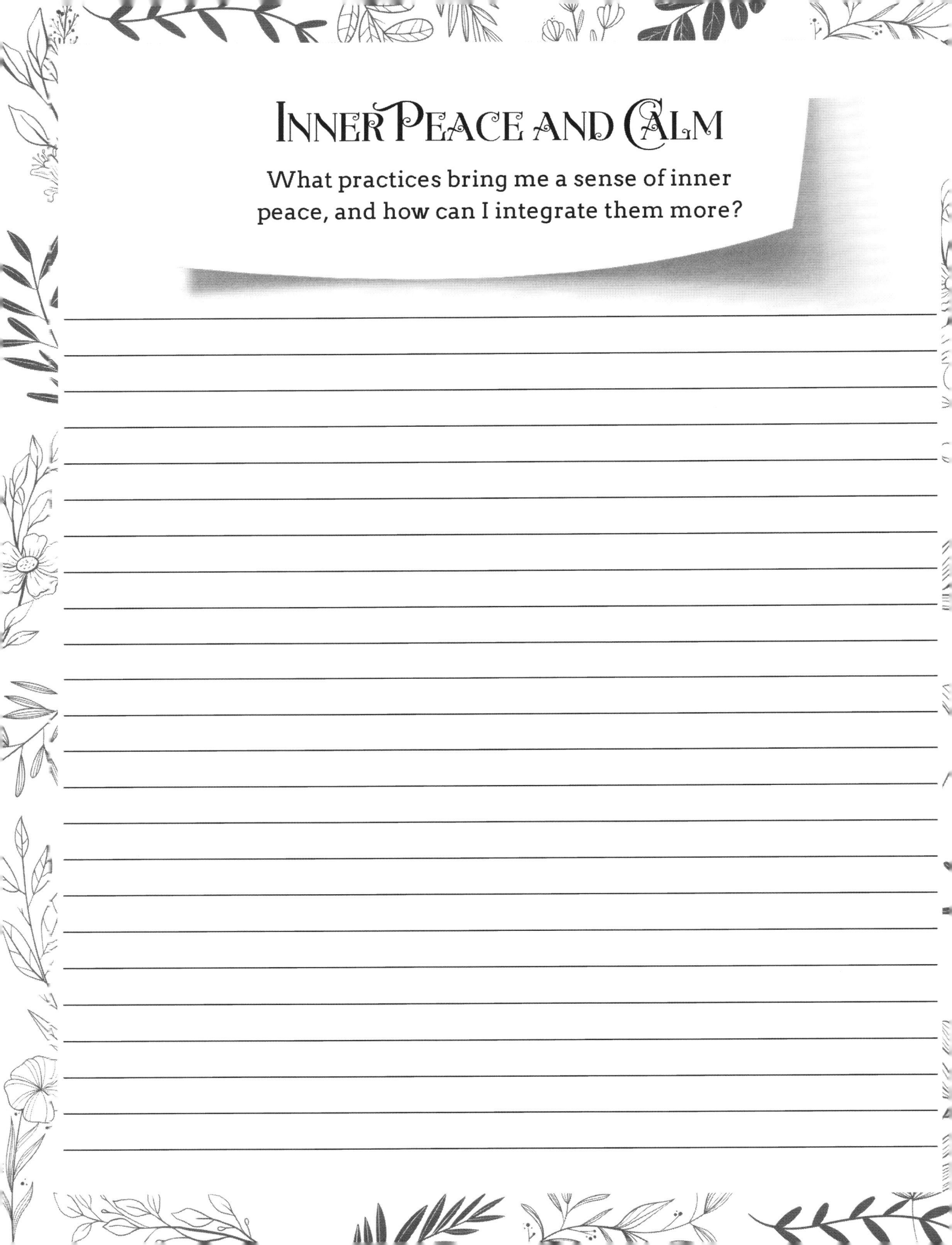

What practices bring me a sense of inner peace, and how can I integrate them more?

# I am calm, centered, and at peace with myself

Inner peace is the quiet strength that guides you, even when life feels chaotic

# I cultivate calm within. I am grounded and at peace

# Self-Care Tips

✓ **Develop a Meditation Practice:** Dedicate time each day to quiet your mind and connect with your inner self.

✓ **Declutter Your Environment:** A calm space can help foster a calm mind, so clear away physical and emotional clutter.

✓ **Accept What You Can't Control:** Focus your energy on what you can change, and release worries beyond your reach.

# Gratitude fills my heart and uplifts my spirit

# Sisterhood & Community

What do you benefit and or desire most from your connections with other women?

# I am surrounded by women who inspire, encourage, and believe in me

"Alone, we can do so little; together, we can do so much."
— Helen Keller

# I strengthen the bonds within my community

# Self-Care Tips

✓ **Reach Out and Connect:** Make time to connect with friends, family, or community members. A simple text, call, or coffee date can strengthen bonds and uplift both of you.

✓ **Celebrate Together:** Organize small gatherings or join group activities that celebrate unity and shared joy. Celebrating with others can deepen your sense of belonging.

✓ **Offer Support and Receive It:** Be open to giving and receiving help. Share your wins, struggles, and goals with your community, creating space for mutual growth and encouragement.

# My journey is enriched by wonderful women beside me

# Divine Feminine Energy

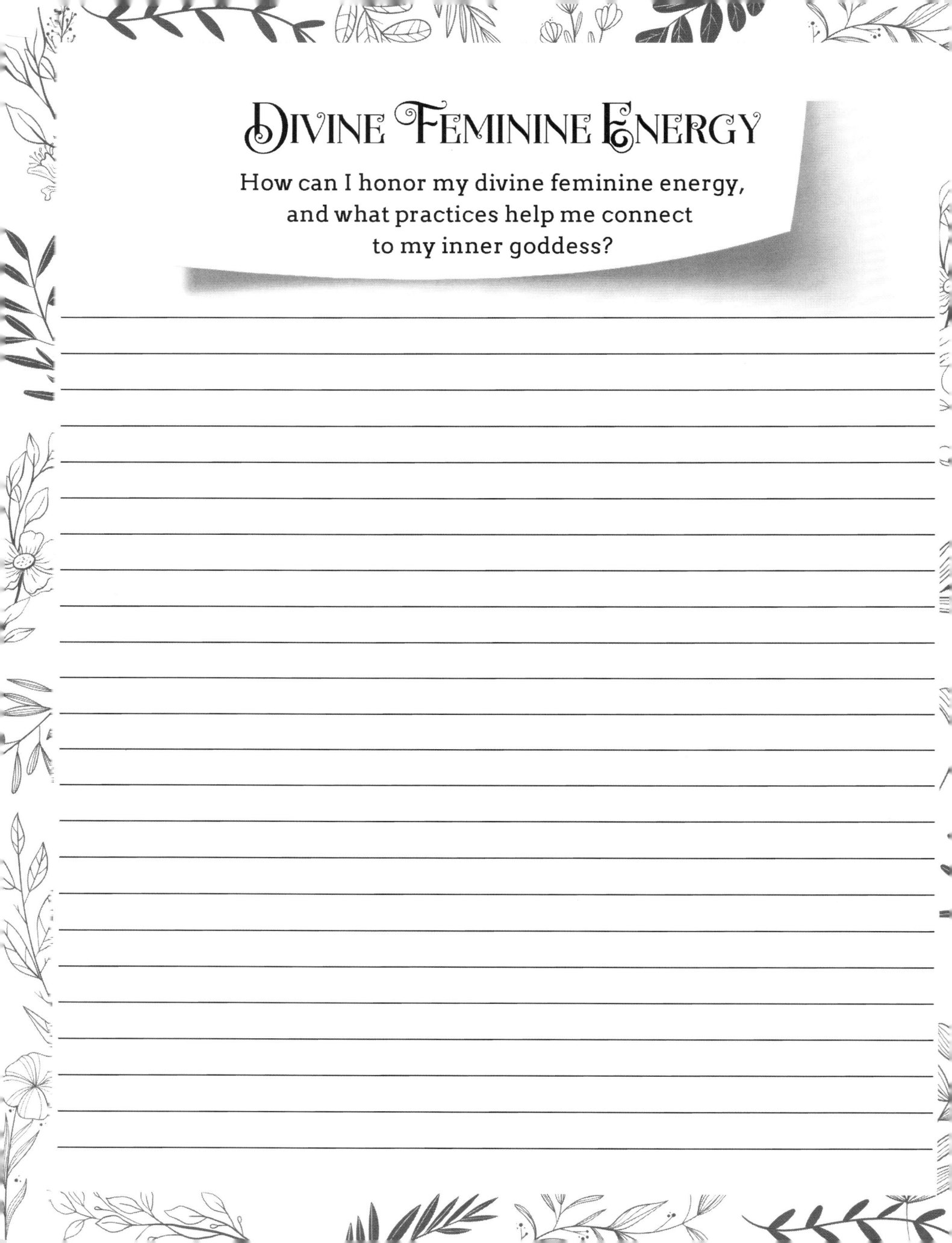

How can I honor my divine feminine energy, and what practices help me connect to my inner goddess?

# I nurture my soul with love and gentleness

The divine feminine is an energy that flows, nurtures, and creates. I am a vessel of wisdom, power, and grace

# I honor my need for rest and relaxation

# Self-Care Tips

✓ **Honor Your Intuition:** Take a few quiet moments daily to listen to your inner voice. Trusting and acting on your intuition helps you stay aligned with your true self.

✓ **Practice Self-Compassion:** Speak kindly to yourself, especially during challenging moments. Embracing softness toward yourself cultivates a powerful, resilient self-love.

✓ **Embrace Rest and Rejuvenation:** Allow yourself time to rest, recharge, and reconnect with your inner being. Gentle practices like meditation, journaling, or mindful breathing can help you reconnect with your core energy.

# I am healing at my own pace, with love and grace

# Healing & Renewal

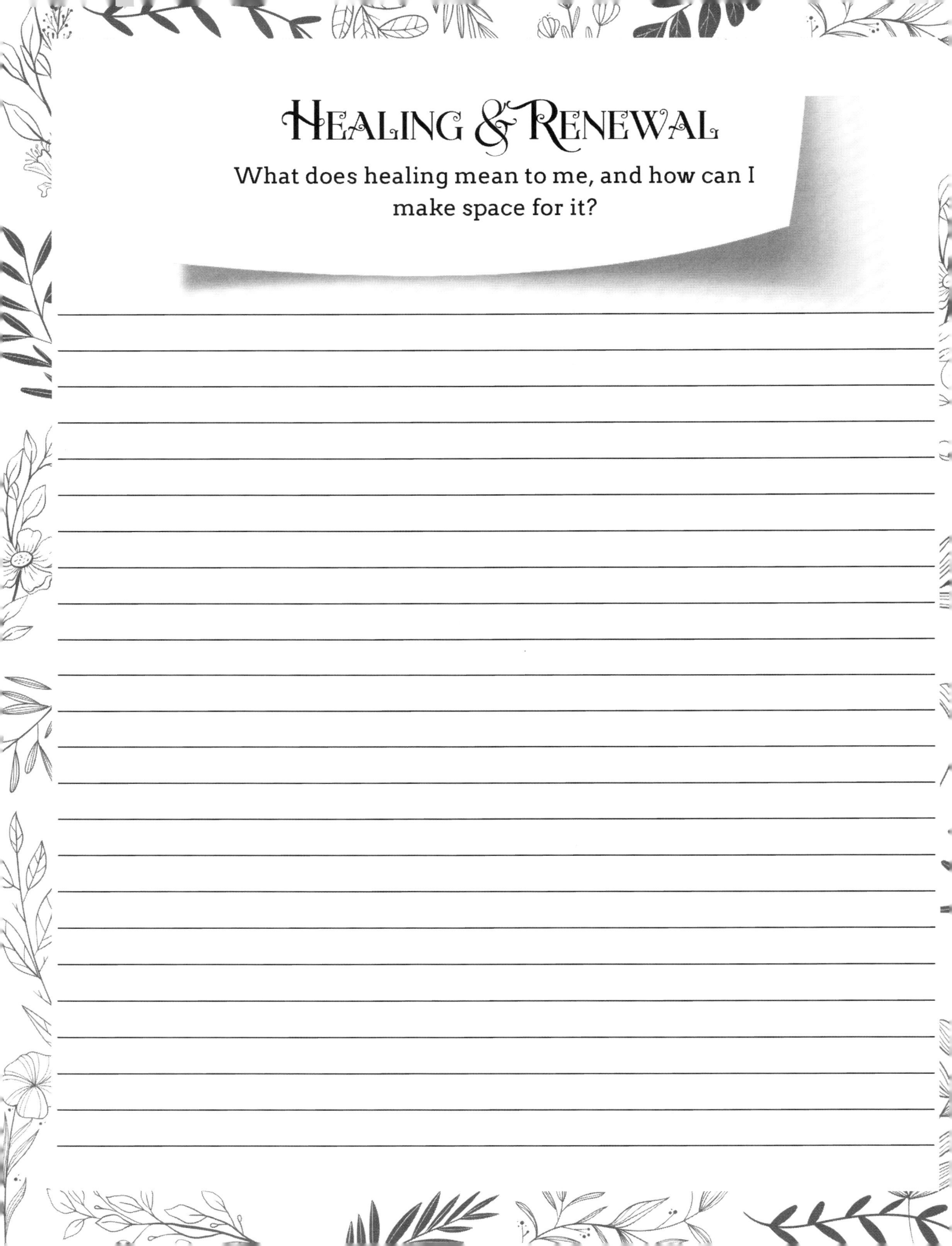

What does healing mean to me, and how can I make space for it?

# My heart is open to love, light, and healing energy

Healing is not a destination; it's a journey of nurturing your soul with patience and love

# My life is filled with purpose and meaning

# Purpose and Passion

What brings me true fulfillment, and how can I pursue my passions with purpose every day?

# I am aligned with my purpose

When I live with purpose and passion, I ignite the world with my unique light

# I welcome joy into every corner of my life

# Joy and Celebration

What simple things bring me joy,
and how can I make more time for them?

# I give myself permission to make time for the things I enjoy

# Self-Care Tips

✓ **Make Time for Play:** Dedicate moments for activities that bring you pure joy and laughter, like dancing or playing games.

✓ **Gratitude Practice:** Keep a journal and write three things that bring you happiness each day.

✓ **Surround Yourself with Positive Energy:** Spend time with people who uplift and energize you.

# I find joy in being fully present in this moment

# Boundaries and Balance

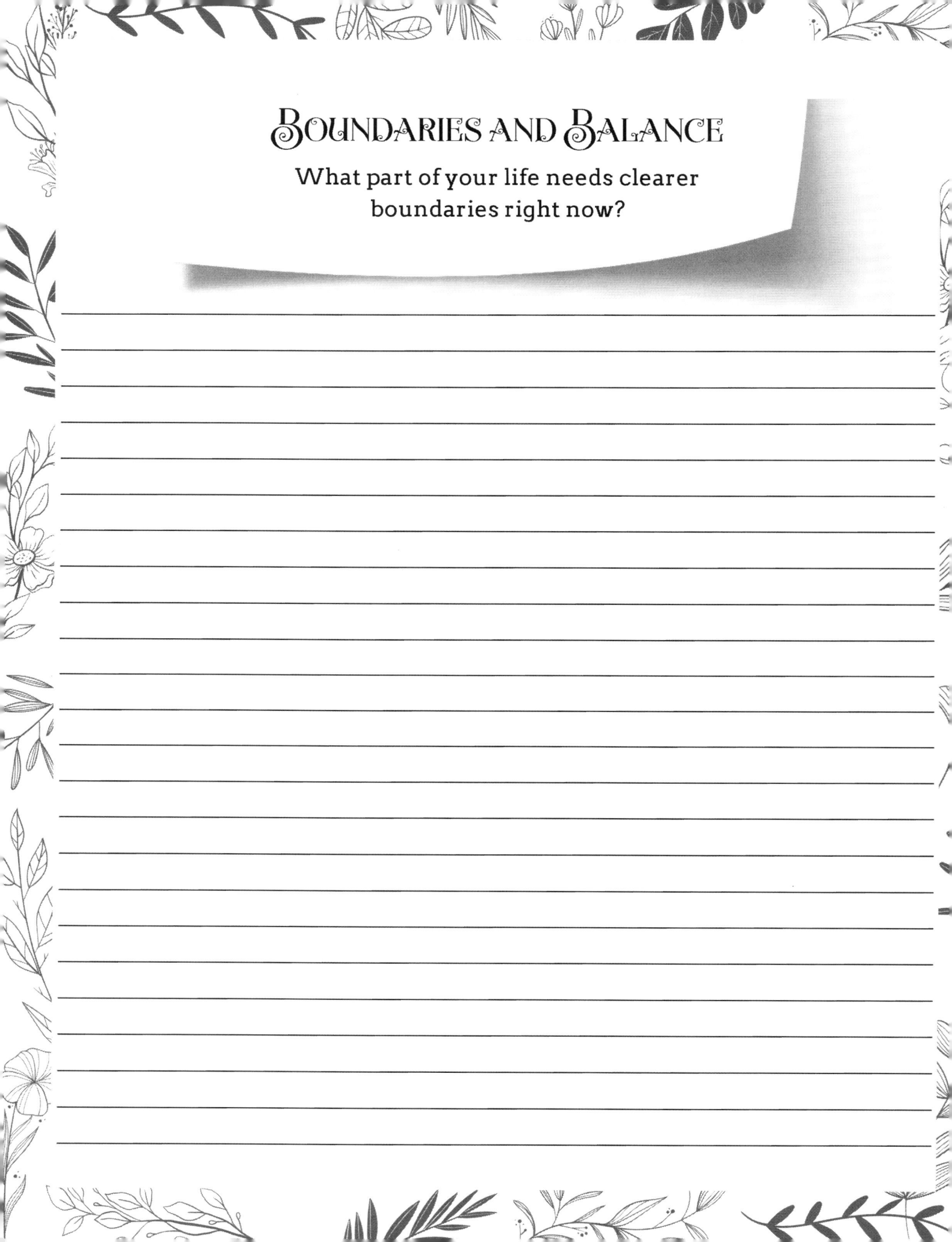

What part of your life needs clearer boundaries right now?

# It's okay to say No to others to say Yes to my well-being

**No**

**Protect**

**Honor**

Balance is not a final destination; it's the dance of honoring each part of your journey

# I embrace the balance that nurtures my soul

# Thank you!

As you reach the final pages of EmpowerHER Soul, take a moment to acknowledge the journey you've just embarked upon. Every stroke, every affirmation, and every reflection has been a step toward a deeper understanding and love for yourself. This book has been a witness to your thoughts, your dreams, your hopes, and perhaps even your healing, and I hope it has reminded you of the infinite beauty and strength within you.

Know that self-love is a continuous journey. Each affirmation, each page, each color was meant to uplift you in moments of doubt and encourage you when you need it most.

Thank you for trusting EmpowerHER Soul to be part of your self-care, for dedicating time to yourself, and for embracing the beauty within. May you continue to shine brightly, inspire others, and walk in the fullness of your own empowerment.

*Ms. Echo*

Made in the USA
Monee, IL
02 December 2024